Hurricane Katrina

Gail
Tuchman

SCHOLASTIC INC.

New York Toronto London Auckland
Sydney Mexico City New Delhi Hong Kong

Read more! Do more!

After you read this book, download your free all-new digital activities.

You can show what a great reader you are!

For Mac and PC

There are lots of interesting things to do!

Take quizzes about the facts in this book.

Log on to
www.scholastic.com/discovermore/readers
Enter this special code: **L2C2RPPHJFP2**

Contents

ISBN 978-0-545-82954-0

12 11 10 9 8 7 6 5 4 3 2 1   15 16 17 18 19 20/0

Printed in the U.S.A.   40
This edition first printing, January 2015

EVACUATION ROUTE

3

Tracking the storm

Hurricane hunter Jack Parrish has flown into 60 hurricanes. He has flown into a hurricane's eye, or center, 523 times! Jack tracks storms before they hit. He lets people know about them.

NEW WORD

eye wall

EYE wawl

The **eye wall** is the ring of thunderstorms around a storm's center.

SAY IT OUT LOUD

This is the storm's eye.

On August 23, 2005, Jack was tracking a storm east of Florida.

"It was early in the storm's life. It was still weak. I flew low, right through the storm's eye wall. It got stronger quickly."

This picture shows the storm near Florida.

The next day, the National Hurricane Center named the storm Katrina. It warned people in southern Florida to be careful. On August 25, Katrina made landfall near Miami, Florida. It was a Category 1 hurricane. This was its first landfall.

NEW WORD

landfall

LAND-fawl

When a hurricane's eye crosses land, the storm has made **landfall**.

SAY IT OUT LOUD

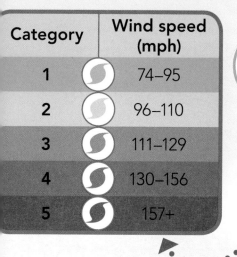

Category	Wind speed (mph)	
1		74–95
2		96–110
3		111–129
4		130–156
5		157+

Date: August 25, 2005
Location: Florida
Wind speed: 80 mph
Status: Category 1

This scale tells people how strong a hurricane is.

When a storm's winds reach 74 mph, it's called a hurricane.

Katrina grew stronger over the next two days. It moved into the Gulf of Mexico. It gained energy from the warm, deep water. Its winds sped up. By August 27, it was Category 3.

Jack Parrish was flying all around Katrina on a high-flying jet.

"I needed to get information to forecast what Katrina would do next. Where was it going? How strong would it be? I soon knew there was nothing that would stop this storm from exploding!"

Date: August 27, 2005
Location: Gulf of Mexico
Wind speed: 115 mph
Status: Category 3

UNITED STATES DEPT. OF COMMERCE

N43RF

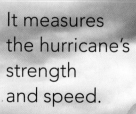

Hurricane hunters always carry high-tech gadgets.

This special tube is dropped into a hurricane.

It measures the hurricane's strength and speed.

By August 28, Hurricane Katrina had doubled in size. Its winds swirled at 175 mph—as fast as a high-speed train.

This giant Category 5 hurricane was now roaring toward New Orleans, Louisiana.

August 25 August 27 August 28

Category 1   Category 3   Category 5

Date: August 28, 2005
Location: Gulf of Mexico
Wind speed: 175 mph
Status: Category 5

First
landfall

LOUISIANA

New
Orleans

FLORIDA

Second
landfall

Miami

GULF OF
MEXICO

KATRINA'S
PATH

Hurricane Katrina was heading for New Orleans. The mayor ordered everyone in the city to evacuate. But many people could not leave. Many were worried about their homes and families.

People lined up to get into the Superdome.

It's a fact!

Over 100,000 people in New

A shelter was set up in the Superdome, the city's sports stadium. Those left behind could wait out the storm there.

Date: August 28, 2005
Location: New Orleans

NEW WORD

evacuate
i-VAK-yoo-ate
When you **evacuate**, you leave a dangerous area.

SAY IT OUT LOUD

Orleans did not evacuate.

13

Katrina strikes!

At 6:10 AM on August 29, Katrina crashed into the Gulf Coast. Its wind speed was 125 mph. It made landfall for the second time 65 miles south of New Orleans. Katrina destroyed towns and cities along the Gulf Coast. Then it moved inland.

Strong winds caused the water to rise. A powerful wall of water pushed onto the shore and hit the land.

It's a fact!

In Pass Christian, Mississippi,

Date: August 29, 2005
Location: Gulf Coast
Wind speed: 125 mph
Status: Category 3

27.8 feet

0 feet

the water was 27.8 feet high.

The storm surge hit New Orleans. The city is like a bowl surrounded by water. There were levees, large earth walls, around it. They were meant to protect the city from flooding.

There is a lake on one side of New Orleans.

New Orleans

levee

But the levees broke.
Water burst through.
It spilled over the levees.
New Orleans was flooded
from both sides.

Date: August 30, 2005
Location: New Orleans

NEW WORD
levee
LEV-ee
The flooding in
New Orleans was
caused mainly by
failed **levees**.
SAY IT OUT LOUD

levee

There is a river
on the other side.

17

New Orleans filled with water.
And the water kept rising. Pumps
to drain the water failed. Soon most
of the city was underwater.

People were still sheltering at the
Superdome. Winds had ripped off
part of the roof. Water leaked in.
There was no power. People were
hungry and thirsty.

People trapped at
home wrote on
their rooftops.

Other people held
on to heavy objects
to stay above water.

The Superdome
was no longer a
safe shelter.

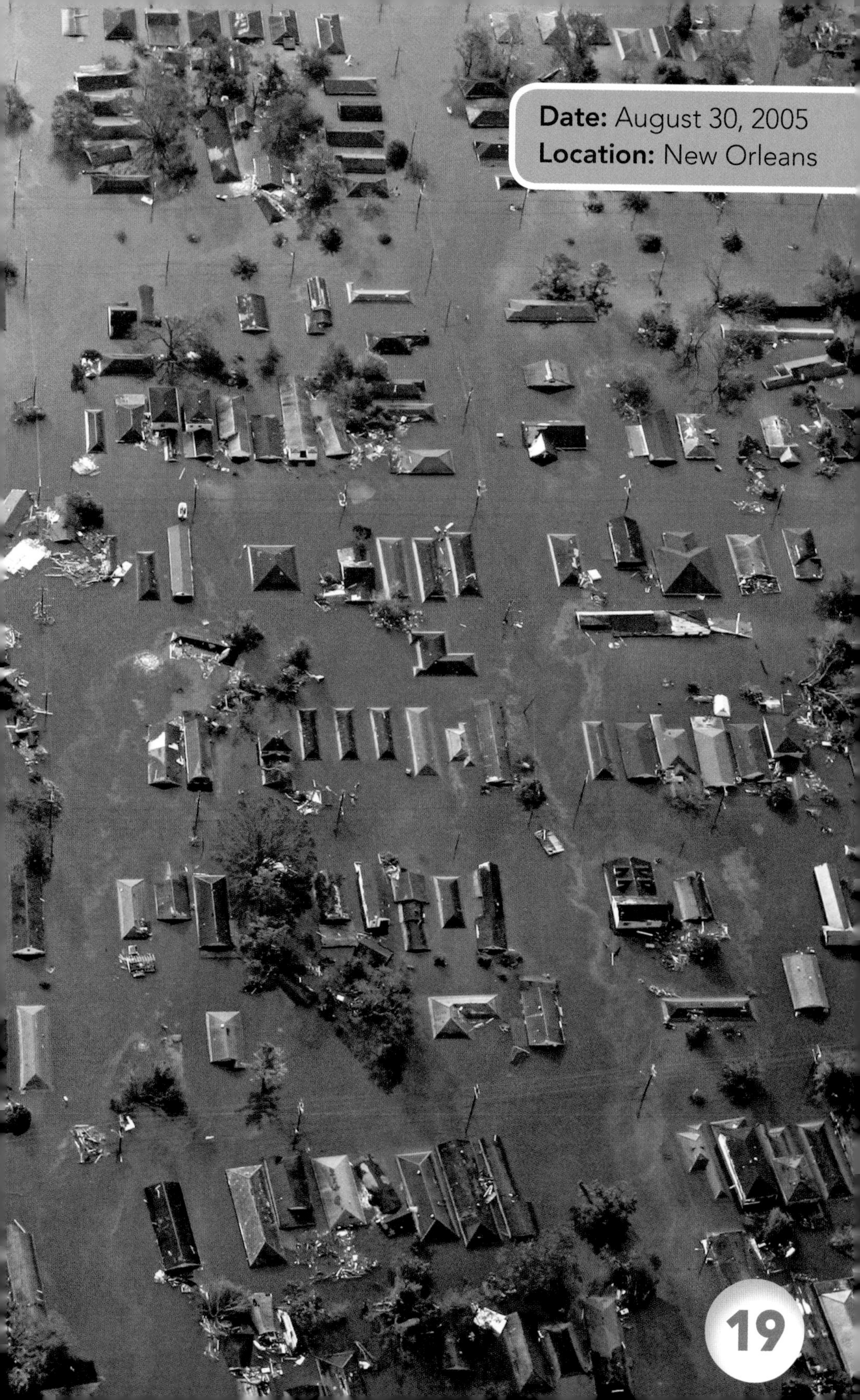

Date: August 30, 2005
Location: New Orleans

To the rescue

Rescue workers searched for people. Helicopters lifted people off roofs. Boats pulled them from the water. Volunteers rushed to help neighbors. The US military was sent in. Many survivors had been rescued by September 5, a week after landfall.

It's a fact!

A 76-year-old man was rescued

The US Coast Guard rescued about 33,000 people.

Many dogs and other pets had to be rescued.

18 days after Katrina hit.

After the hurricane

It took about five weeks to drain New Orleans and nearby areas of 250 billion gallons of water! People began to return to their homes a month after Katrina had hit the city.

Geranika Richardson, then age 12, cried when she came back to her old house.

"It was so quiet and dark, no lights, no people, no birds, no animals. It was like a ghost town. It smelled and you didn't hear anything."

People started to rebuild their lives. Dave and Judy Walker went back to work.

"Judy and I write for a New Orleans newspaper. Katrina is still in stories I write. After Katrina, Judy asked people to send in old family recipes. This helped other people replace recipes swept away by the flood. They could save this important part of their history."

Rebuilding homes

2005

2014

25

Looking ahead

No one will forget Hurricane Katrina. In the Gulf Coast area, 1,836 people lost their lives. Over 1 million homes were damaged. But the floodwaters could not wash away the strength and spirit of the people of New Orleans.

Recovering from the hurricane has been a long and painful process. But today New Orleans is alive and hopeful!

Katrina in numbers

Here are some facts and figures about Katrina.

8 dolphins were rescued 2 weeks after being swept out of a water park.

1.2 million people left the New Orleans area in the days before Katrina landed.

504 vessels ended up on dry land.

Hurricane Katrina struck **90,000** square miles of land.

7.4 million gallons of oil poured into the water.

The levees protecting New Orleans failed in at least **50** places.

60,000 people could not get out of their homes. They stayed in attics or on roofs until they were rescued.

80% of New Orleans was underwater.

68 million meals and snacks were given out by Red Cross volunteers.

25,000 people took shelter at the Superdome.

Hurricane Katrina caused a lot of damage. It cost **$96–$125 billion**.

Glossary

damage
The harm caused by something. To be damaged is to be harmed.

drain
To remove water from something or somewhere.

evacuate
To leave a dangerous area or building.

eye
The calm, clear area at the center of a hurricane.

eye wall
The ring of thunderstorms around the eye of a hurricane.

flood
To overflow with water.

forecast
To say what will happen in the future.

gadget
A small tool that does a special job.

Gulf Coast
The part of the coast of the United States that is on the Gulf of Mexico. The states on the Gulf Coast are Texas, Louisiana, Mississippi, Alabama, and Florida.

Gulf of Mexico
An area of the Atlantic Ocean that is bordered by the United States to the north and Mexico to the south.

hurricane
A violent, swirling storm with heavy rain and strong winds. Hurricanes form over warm waters.

inland
Away from the sea.

landfall
The point at which a hurricane's eye crosses land after being over water.

levee
A large earth wall near water, built to keep the area around it from flooding.

National Hurricane Center
An organization that forecasts and tracks storms so that it can warn people if a storm is coming.

process
A series of actions or events. Recovering after a disaster is a process.

recover
To get better after a disaster, an accident, or sickness.

Red Cross
An organization that helps people who are in trouble after a disaster.

rescue
To save someone who is in danger.

roar
To rush loudly.

shelter
A place that protects people from bad weather or danger. To shelter somewhere is to go to a place where it is safe.

storm surge
A rise in sea level caused by a storm. Storm surges can cause flooding.

survivor
Someone who lives through a disaster.

swirl
To move with a twisting motion.

track
To follow the path of something, such as a storm.

vessel
A ship or boat.

volunteer
A person who does a job without being paid for it.

Index

Images
Alamy Images: 16 c, 17 c (FEMA), 14 main, 15 main (Jim Reed/RGB Ventures/SuperStock), 27 fg (Jim West); AP Images/Bill Haber: cover house; Corbis Images: cover dog on car (Lee Celano/Reuters), 6, 7 (Mike Theiss/Ultimate Chase), 18 bc (Robert Galbraith/Reuters), 18 bg, 19 (Smiley N. Pool/Dallas Morning News); David Walker: 24 b inset; Dreamstime: 3 bl (Americanspirit), cover sky (Bcon Management Inc.), 22, 23 bg (Briannolan), 16 t sky, 17 t sky (Cristian Nitu), hurricane symbol throughout (Fintastique), 3 b bg (Les Cunliffe), 10 bg, 11 bg (Michael Schmeling), 8 bg, 9 bg (Mikko Pitkänen/Alias Studiot Oy), 28 bl (Ramon Berk), 24 t sky (Tatyana Vychegzhanina); DVIDS/USCG: 32 b fg; FEMA: 29 bl; Geranika Richardson: 23 inset; Getty Images: 20 b inset (Mario Tama), 26, 27 bg (Mario Villafuerte/Bloomberg), 18 bl (Robert Galbraith/AFP), 20 bg, 21 bg (Vincent Laforet/AFP); iStockphoto: 28 tl (A-Digit), 29 cr (Alex Belomlinsky), 28 crt (ChrisGorgio), 15 family icon (filo), 29 br (Genericamerican0), inside front cover tr (Kathy Konkle), inside front cover br (lushik), 28 tr (matsiash), 28 br (mevans), 15 house icon (miniature), 2 cursor arrow (papadesign), 32 bg (PattieS), cartoon weatherwoman throughout (rhoon), inside front cover c (seamartini), back cover b, 2 computer monitor (skodonnell), tape throughout (spxChrome), 16 cityscape icon, 17 cityscape icon (Yurkaimmortal); Landov/The Times-Picayune: 20 b fg, 25 t, 25 b (John McCusker); 12 main, 13 (Ted Jackson); Media Bakery/Jim West: 24 b bg; NASA: 10 b (Goddard Space Flight Center Scientific Visualization Studio), 11 c hurricanes (Jeff Schmaltz, MODIS Land Rapid Response Team), 1 (Jeff Schmaltz, MODIS Rapid Response Team, GSFC), 4, 5 bg (Mike Trenchard, Earth Sciences & Image Analysis Laboratory, Johnson Space Center), 9 br; National Center for Atmospheric Research: 9 br inset l; NOAA: 5 bl (Mike Trenchard, Earth Sciences & Image Analysis Laboratory, Johnson Space Center), back cover t, 3 t bg, 3 cr, 5 br, 8 b, 9 c, 9 br inset r, 30, 31; US Navy/Photographer's Mate Airman Jeremy L. Grisham: 18 br; US Air Force: 9 bc (Senior Airman Anna-Marie Wyant), 9 bl (Staff Sgt. Randy Redman); US Coast Guard: 28 crb, 29 cl, 29 tr.

Thank you
For their generosity of time in sharing their experiences of Katrina, special thanks to Alicia Little, Jack Parrish, Geranika Richardson, and Dave and Judy Walker. Thank you also to Phyllis C. Hunter.